Glitter Out

Copyright (C) 2020 Lori Moilov

All rights reserved.
Published in the United States, by Make the Honey Publishing, a division of Make the Honey entertainment media.

Library of Congress Cataloging-in-Publishing Data
Moilov, Lori
Glitter Out
Poetry

Printed in the United States of America

ISBN: 978-1-67813-432-7

Book design and Cover design by Lori Moilov
About author picture by Lily Yorke

10 9 8 7 6 5 4 3 2 1
First Paperback Edition

Introduction

It all started as a splash of inspiration! I want this poem book to be that splash of glitter on a page where no matter what poem you read, you leave shining, and above all happy. I love poetry. Growing up I was addicted to Shakespeare and "A light in the Attic" by Shel Silverstein. In 2017 I was shooting "The Doors 50th" with a photographer friend, Jill Jarret. She got me a shirt at the Malibu Guitar Festival it was an original Doors shirt with Jim Morrison on it. Jim was known as not only as an amazing artist, but also great poet, which reignited my interest in poetry. I started wearing the shirt and a friend in Long Beach for a long time, Philosophy kept inviting me to poetry sessions. I caved and started sharing some poems that I was creating. I immediately was hooked! It evolved in helping me with my storytelling and songwriting process. I hope with these poems to splash you with a touch of glitter. And that it touches you to be inspired to follow your dreams and make them come true. Each poem is a piece of my heart and soul, I hope it resonates and moves you to create your perfect masterpieces. I want you to know that patience, passion, and persistence is always the key. I BELIEVE IN YOU! May these poems help you shine and help you "Glitter Out" sharing your talents with the world!

PEACE & LOVE ~ Lori Moilov

Special thanks to Diane Warren for your encouraging words. Also, a big thanks to my family, friends, and collaborators for their continuous love and support.

Poems:

1. Love is Blind
2. Struggling Movement
3. Planting a Seed
4. Surface
5. Encouragement
6. Sky is the limit
7. Faith
8. Creativity
9. Imagination
10. Human
11. Find you
12. Selfie
13. One love
14. Masterpiece
15. Unity
16. Smiles
17. You are all stars to me
18. Visions
19. Make time
20. Challenges
21. WOW
22. Dreams
23. Roots
24. Scars
25. Running

26. Magic
27. Pursuit
28. Go with your gut
29. Drive
30. Room to grow
31. Goals
32. Dance
33. Vibes
34. It's within
35. Passion
36. Relax
37. Creation
38. Friendships
39. Play
40. New Beginnings
41. The world in our hands
42. Enslaved
43. Rebirth
44. Fearless
45. Patience
46. Keep pushing towards goals
47. Last shot
48. Human vs. Machine
49. Heal
50. There is always time
51. Depression
52. Synchronicity
53. Originality
54. Happiness

55. Focus
56. Freedom
57. Transformation
58. Impact
59. Simplicity
60. Consistency
61. Beauty
62. Serendipity
63. Secrets
64. Motivations
65. Value
66. Lucky luck
67. Destiny
68. Never say never
69. Leadership
70. Instinct
71. Recalibrate
72. Resilience
73. New perspectives
74. Spark
75. Reinvent
76. Confidence
77. Desires
78. Legacy
79. Vibrations
80. Magnetic
81. Enlightened People
82. Finding what you need
83. Falling in

84. Rejection
85. Courageous
86. The moment we are timeless
87. Hope
88. Dream Puff
89. Angel in the outfield
90. Let me be your wings
91. Enthusiasm
92. Manifesting
93. Lead with love
94. New memories
95. Time traveler
96. Brave
97. Soul digger
98. Glitter
99. Be the best version of YOU
100. Find your slice of Heaven

Love is BLIND

Love is a perspective
No lens in a frame
Just a pure feeling
Matchstick to a flame
Burning
Pumping, heart thumping, showers of rain
Trying to understand it in my brain
Desires, fires, feed by endless blood in my veins
This feeling, this feeling
Hard to describe
Everyone needs to prescribe
No labels to define
Hearts intertwined
Love is blind, Love is blind
Close your eyes as they deceive
Love is endless if you just believe
Doesn't matter how you look
Never judge the cover of a book
The outside is a shell
Souls like a pulse knocking at your doorbell
Wake up, Wake up
You can finally see
From seed to root love is a tree
Growth and layers of depth
No need to suffocate you can breathe

No barriers to breed
This is what a heart needs
Kisses and hugs to show me
How deep you see
The way you hold me
Forgiving in sight
Your love is my light
No lists to the height
We can go anywhere
Nothing can compare
Unconditional
Untraditional
Limitless love
When you just take my breath away
Abundance of love you can't outweigh
Love with no hesitation
Words hard to find the sensation
No reasons
No seasons
Love is blind, Love is blind
No more blindfold all I want is you to hold
Life
Over
Varied
Emotions
With all hearts open

Struggling movement

The pain I disdain
Holds
Carrying scars
Fears
Trying to license my intuition
Judgments
For being afraid of what they see
Losing sight of the picture of me
Trying to fit a mold
Trying to do what I'm told
Hostage
Just in the fear of being me
Inside my head
Way too much then
Taking steps back and forth
Questioning my course
Tortured inside
Fighting it trying to run and hide
Looking out for signs to be my guide
Where to go
How will I know
Show me
Answers aren't so clear
How did I get here
Past present future
Life's ride is my teacher

Learning from mistakes
Outgrowing the image of fake
Keeping it all so real
Who cares if those around can't deal
My struggle
I feel
Pain torture in my brain
Trying to not go insane
Hitting a turn in the road
Enlightening my soul
A new day to be whole
The pieces once shattered
Now a memory a reminder a hazard
Don't look back you see
Holding on was the problem to be
Creating it suffocating it with my pressure
Release it and jump into adventure
Stop holding on and set free
No more struggles
Just be
To move in the sea
No matter the waves and current
Step outside and have the courage
A struggle once there is now gone
Time to just go on
Your struggle doesn't confine you
It just was a moment to define you

To push you out
Without a doubt
To be the best you
Bring light to your truth

Planting a seed

A seed placed
Dug up in a deep space
Fighting to see light
No sight
Hiding in the dark
With tender care
Water comes
Falls
Light and hydration starts to seep
Growth starts to happen when everyone is asleep
Starting to expand
Feeling grand
Finally exposed to light
Growing bigger and bigger, day and night
Taking root
Soul breaking thru
Peeking out to the sun, starting to bear fruit
Dealing with all conditions coming
Rain, sunshine, and lighting
It stands
From seed, root, and finally a flower
Blossoms with beauty, that is it's Power
See we are all a seed
Needing a little TLC
To grow into what we are suppose to be
No matter the conditions

Expanding our love is our ammunition
To finally grow to be that great tree
Ready to radiate wild and free

Surface

How do we look past
What is presented in front of us
Perception
Illusions
A game
Played on the brain
Images defining what we think is everything
It doesn't even etch the surface
The root, the pulse, the heart
Small talk
Like lost darts
Always missing the mark
Because we need to dig deeper
Have compassion
Not look at what is at a first glance
Look past, look past
Everyone has a story
All needs love to feel fulfilled
Opening up is the first step to build
Real relationships
Not superficial mind trips
Stop focusing on materials to give our glory
Our hidden gem is our life story
Who we are and what we do
That is the measuring cup to live to
Where do you begin

It starts when you finally are comfortable in your own skin
Time to open up
Reach out and you will see
The surface was just a exterior
Truth always was in the interior
Everyone has much more to give
A channel to tune in to and live
Just start to dig

Encouragement

Inspired by Diane

Words stack up
Putting pressure how to measure up
Imprinted in our minds
The words pressed upon to make us more defined
To build or tear down everything in their path
At just one glance
The power they hold
Behold
You can listen either to the lies told
Or watch the truth unfold
Daggers of negativity fed
It was inbred
They harm as they have been harmed
Don't be alarmed
It is just perspective
The words they played ineffective
Real words for encouragement set fire
A way to build empires
With hearts desires
A champion to inspire
A spark
That ignites
Dreams taken to higher heights
For the words we use hold power

Either to inspire or devour
So in our finest hour
Remember it's power
Encourage
Watch as dreams flourish
One word, one touch, one smile
One to change the world with style
A game changer
Not a naysayer
To hold words up as a main player
Keep spreading kindness and joy
Be true take life's ride and enjoy
Keep encouraging others
To illuminate all the colors
Key is to persist
Listen to the kind words, I insist
Keep building, keep running, keep going
You never know the magic that exists
Let spirits lift, we each have a gift
So light it
Help others find it
Not deny it
Shine it
You have it
Sisters brothers fathers mothers
Friends
Encourage each other

Sky is the limit
It's understood
Under the stars
With your head in the clouds
Anything is possible
Nothing is impossible
You can go far beyond the reach
Get out of your way
No brakes
Keep pushing ahead anyway
No limits
No gimmicks
The sky is the limit

Faith

The storm has come and gone
It felt like everything was going wrong
Head down
Trying to figure out what to do now
Lost in a sea of emotions
Confused in the vast oceans
Finding a way to not sink
Feeling on the edge of the brink
Hurt from the past
Holding me with every grasp
I couldn't go back
Never wanted any of that
Always measuring
Old things kept pestering
Realized
I needed to recognize
It was all a part of my mind
Making me blind
Playing tricks
Hitting me like bricks
All this weight
Being put on the brakes
The only way to get out was to put it in faith
Not just pray
But to do something today
The thought and belief

I could do anything to achieve
Being touched by a higher being
Looking at the sky hearing angels singing
Cloaked
Soaked
Thought provoked
This new feeling and mindset
Put me in the sky
To finally believe and achieve to greater heights imaginable
This new feeling of faith feels incredible

Creativity

Forced or not
Creativity exists
Where parallel lines twist
Creating a place
Transcendence in time and space
Lightning strikes with deep passion
In all types of fashions
Paintbrush, pencil, pen, all to a page
Rushing to capture this creative rampage
For when it hits
You don't have a moment to miss
Feeling like it won't happen again
Trying to contain
At any time it could strike
Even at the stroke of midnight
Instead
Focus on all the gems
In every moment
Keep focused, you are chosen
The pure genius is it is happening every time
There is a real true crime
We don't allow ourselves to be creative enough
Hands bound in handcuffs
Set your mind free
You will see
Creativity in everything

Unbound by anything
Look around
Sky to ground
Nature to humanity
Magically
Every moment can inspire
Take a breath in and admire
Your environment
Your thoughts
You can set fire to create
Never stagnate
It is all around you
Just start creating
Activating
New ways of captivating
Any form
To inform
A way to share imagination
Electric, eccentric, vibration
The beauty of creation

Imagination

Where do you begin to create
A idea turned into a landscape
An area where you can pretend to be
A way to create a legacy
Outside of the box
Echoing inside thoughts
That finally reach a surface
Flowing full of greatness busting out the curtains
Pure play
Spinning around like the perfect ballet
Even outer space
The Birthplace
Where it all comes together woven
Great sea of ideas flowing like the ocean
Nonstop
Only way is up to the top
Perspectives
With no bounds
A blank canvas
From an idea to anything can happen
Imagination where nothing is lacking if you just open your
inner dragon

Human

Illuminate a light
Even at night
For when we are wrong
We sometimes feel so right
Mistakes
Wrongdoing
For sometimes our ignorance causes harm
Not knowing that we have hurt others on our path
In our sadness and wrath
Not understanding the hurt we have caused
Wishing we should of held back and paused
Taken a moment
Seeing the pictures before it unfolded
But our emotions played a role
Took over and took control
We replicated the mere action that struck a nerve
Pushing upon vibrations no one deserves
In the heat of a moment
You should not have spoken
Or taken that action
That caused a continuous chain reaction
One after another back and forth
A saga, cycle of rebirth
Happening again and again
Trying to make it all end
Our reactions and words

Thrown as distractions for the birds
When the real line of communication exists
Opening one's mind and soul are the gifts
To share and be heard by those you love
Has more meaning than all of the above
We lose track
And always forget all of that
For we are all human
Forget the sidetracked illusions
Connection is our movement
Blooming
Booming
Music
Moving
We are just human

Find you

Like a window not a door
Open your heart
Look into the mirror
And let love soar
Life is not easy, but you better let the world hear you roar
Your voice counts
Your touch matters
You never know who you will affect
Just sharing a piece of you
Don't hold back and be true
Regardless the cost
Don't feel lost
Each time you lose sight
The only way is
Positive vibes to invite
Search within
You have so much to give
Just be you
Yourself

Selfie

Obsessed
An addict
Hooked on self portraits
Life distorted
Consumed by the fact that the world centers around myself
Putting those around me on a bookshelf
These relationships collect dust
But it is my self-centered addiction that I must
In that moment of trust
Take a picture extending my arm and snapping to post
Instead of living in the moment with friends laughing, I gone ghost
Absent and obsessed to share what I'm doing instead of being in it
Live in the moment, I say, but feeling like a hypocrite
What happened to the days of the past
Polaroid
Captured and printed in an instant
Now that instant not so instant
And the only thing besides an abundance of selfies is the distance
That road we created away from others
Disconnecting
Illusions of connecting
Sharing sharing sharing
Instead of enjoying each other

Too consumed
Assumptions presumed
By images false or real creating our realities
Hooked on social like a disease
Every moment we want to capture and squeeze
Forgetting we lost the moment by not being present
Lost in the sea of selfie content
You
Me
Everybody
Addicted
Real connections drifted
Put the phone down
And touch each others souls
With a smile or helping hand
No more selfies
Be in the moment
Self-less
Care-free
You don't need to capture everything
A space to bring
All of you no WiFi attached
Time to detach
Be relaxed
It's just a moment you get to breath in
Finally be in your skin
Phones, computers, and technology away

Room for intimate connections to make way
Touch
See
Experience with all of you
You will feel the difference that our parents felt
Life with no seat belt
Living on the edge
Connecting with real friends
Not playing pretend
Excited where it can go
Talking about moments
Not texting or sending screenshots
Bitmojis and talking about being a
Snapchat bot
Things that exist without being shared
With those close that really care
Self present here
No devices raw moments to share
Not on any social
Just a witness trying to be hopeful
Real connections viral and global

One love

You never know about that one life you can change
Your heart always beats
Never mark defeat
Through the struggle is when our greatest moments happen
You look in the mirror awaken and realize nothing is lacking
You step outside your doorstep
Step by step
You finally love the shoes you accept
A smile you pass by
A look
A energy emotes
One love it evokes
We are all one
To embrace and love
Purpose to give the world a hug
Share our heart open up
There is so much to give up
Get rid of the fears
Just love, even if it brings tears
They are ones of joy
When all hearts beat in sequence
That pulse is infinite
One is all it takes
To make the world a better place
You are that one

Never forget
You can move mountains
Love spouting
See the change
One by one
Spreading
A change that is happening
It starts with you
Walk out in your truth
Smile
Hug
Love
We need more propel change
Hate, war, and lack of love creates us to disengage
Connect and love is the best way to make a great change
One action
One smile
One person
One love
Creates a chain reaction

Masterpiece

Slow moving as a tortoise
Or moving fast with purpose
Either way it's a stroke on canvas
Painting light and taking chances
A moment to breathe in creation
To express all of worlds creations
Illuminated by touch, sight, taste, and sound
Orbiting all around
Inspiration strikes
All forms all types
Words to visions
Start to take flight
Daylight then tonight creating is our birthright
Each of us artists in motion
Vast seas of inspiration that is as big as the ocean
Illustrating images and sounds to create a masterpiece
A burst of colors to release
Each creation inspiring the next
Simple or complex it connects
We all have the touch
Our tools in our minds and hands
Keep painting, once done it will be grand
No matter how quick or long it takes
Your work can create earthquakes
To move mountains and minds
To be woven in space

Tapestry not only you can see, feel, hear, and taste
Tap into your mastermind
And just spill out your glitter and shine
Everything you create awakens your unspoken divine
Find it, make it, and keep creating ripples shaping moments in time
Keep creating and be at peace
You are a masterpiece

Unity

Great Minds, transcend time
Through connection
Connecting the dots of the universe together
All people even through all the pressure
A place where worlds constantly collide
Different perspectives from yours to mine
But our insight to come together instead of divide
All so different
Each of our cultures, religions, and minds all so magnificent
Blending it together to make magic
Unity, where peace and happiness can happen
Forces of change
I have a dream
Can take space
To create
To flourish
To define new possibilities
All with the ability
Shaping different perspectives to come as one
When we all come together everything can be won
Undeniable we
Now can
Ignite
Togetherness
Yes we can
United we stand for unity

Smiles

One can frown
One can hold their head down
But in the shift of a moment
A peek of a smile keeps growing
Radiating energy
Creating a world of synergy
For it starts to grow from a laugh
Millions being captured by a photograph
Spreading
One by one
Smiles start to hit everyone
Shifting the vibe
Making all feel alive
As it is just a matter of being
Happy
A joyous moment to share
Feeling like a billionaire
Just one smile is all it takes
To create a ripple effect, earthquake
Keep smiling and watch it take fire
As one by one we all have the power to inspire
Through a smile a window to the soul
To help each other illuminate and glow
Keep smiling
Inspiring
It is exciting

You are all stars to me
Under the sky
Wind blowing
Not knowing
The future
In control
Destiny
Deep thought and intensity
Laying and staring at the dark sky
Asking all lives mysteries, who, what, and why
Shining and flashing lights in the distance
Trying to understand mere existence
Shooting stars
Healing Scars
Pondering
Wondering
Dreaming
Imagination, sparking good feelings
Thinking of everyone
I'm orbiting
A mini-universe
You are all stars to me
Consultations
Clusters of light
Spreading
Illuminating through day and night
Just keep shining

Stop hiding
Your star will twinkle
You are that diamond, keep your sparkle
For you all are stars meant to shine bright
Awaken and share your light

Visions

Sometimes what you see
Is just one side
Glass half empty
Or half full
But, it never was about the glass
It was about seeing past all of that
It was about how you were about to use this glass and
What was in it
To make some magic
Make time
We make excuses
But we don't make time
Time for those that matter
Time for those we care about
Time wasted on small doubts
What if we shifted in our mind to make time
Time to awaken and make priorities
Always getting distracted normally
Focus on what matters and watch it grow
Let your care and compassion seep through and show
There are too many things to do in a day
It's impossible, but when you simplify it all
You will see I am possible
So make that time for you
And the ones you care about before time runs out
My time to make time, now

Challenges

Hurdles
Trying to jump over them all
Sometimes stumbling and taking a fall
But you must dust off and get back up
As you never know what can startup
If you just push past
Keep going, slow or fast
The hardest part is taking that chance
But it becomes easy step by step advance
Even in adversity
Even with no certainty
Out of necessity
Be brave that is your currency
To stand against all odds
That moment will come where you get applauds
For you took that risk when no one else would
Misunderstood by the outside world
But you knew you were going to press past and do some good
Challenges are just a mere test
To shape you into your best
Be strong
And carry on

Wow

Any moment can take a breath away
Be ready
Be prepared
Stop subjecting yourself to the torture of what everyone else thinks
Just don't care
Only you know what it takes to be wowed
It is all possible
Dreams to reality
Anything can happen is a guarantee
Just be amazed what you will see
Believe, dream, beyond Reach
Doesn't look possible unless you believe
Anything you can imagine and conceive
You must keep looking for what you seek
If it isn't there, the lesson is always something to teach
To grow and become anything
Doesn't matter where you come from
Past is not your present
Be patient and know your intent
Strive for what you want
Just be confident
All dreams await
Time to paint and create
The canvas is yours to take
Be bold make earthquakes

Roots

The roots dig deep in the soil
Taking hold of the ever-shifting ground
Baring no exposure to light
Knowing it will hold everything together above sight
Spreading to create more growth
Energy good or bad, holds both
It's ability to grasp into the dirt and earth
From a seed spreads to give birth
Small movements constantly
Beating all odds consistently
Roots are the expansion of our minds we choose the energy it holds
Be aware of the roots you take
As it will either make you strong or weak
It's all in what you radiate and speak
Stay grounded to your soul
You are a conductor, a magnetic pole
Strike, lightning bolt
But roots under always grounded
Think of the words you define inner and outer, you are surrounded
Drench yourself in radiance
And just dance with the wind
All storms past
Now is time to dance

Scars

Scars are the reminders of the pain
But you don't have to live in it
As a open wound becomes healed
It is now stitched and sealed
Not like it was never there
But meant to show you what was repaired
We forget
Lose track
Sometime wish they were gone
But they show us what we did wrong
Or they chose us
A guide to help make sure we don't go down the misguided path
A symbol of how you survived through the aftermath
With strength you healed and must be brave
Otherwise fear has you stuck enslaved
Lessons learned
Reminded remembered
By your scars help stitch you back whole
To remind you of your heart and soul
Running
So many times before I have run
Too much on my mind with no sight at fun
Problems after problems
I just kept trying to solve them
Like a traveler in the night on the run

But the truth was every action was a trigger switch firing the gun
Moment to moment everything determined
All by the actions and mindsets feeling burdened
Running around and around
Losing sight of the ground
Head in the clouds
No noise yet screams in my mind so loud
How to stop it
Make it quit
The only thing I could think was to run away from it
Forget it all
Not focus on my fall
But, it keeps coming back
There was a lesson
I had to learn how to react
Instead of run face the truth
You know what to do
Stop running and just be
You will see
The magic inside of you and me
No conflict just elevating
No escalating
Just levitating ideas
Pure freedom
No time to run
Just put yourself out there and have a little fun

Magic

Inspired by a class at the songwriting school of LA

Healing is like a baton
A wand, striking magic
Bounces, flipping imagination to reach the stars
As it strikes light it shines
Synchronized playing and laughter
Floating smiles and joy
Like a balloon set free
Creating bliss for everybody
Ice cream trees brushing in the wind
When it twinkles sparkling even in the dark
While kids play it seeks realness
Bonding each other like glue
Attracting each like magnets to it's magic
Pixie dust and batons
Bringing all together to bond
To help afflictions with great intuition
Spreading one by one
Impacting everyone
Collisions of ideas happening
Blossoming thoughts and wishes
Dreams and vivid children at play
Where magic happens always

Pursuit

When the only option you have
It's not just a chance
It is a mission
To take a thought to a vision
That moment that defines a movement
A progression
Creative expression
Expands minds
Builds to the end of time
One seed to another
Growing to love each other
Understanding
Compassion
In the pursuit of our passions
To shine from our love
To become anything you dream of
The challenge it takes
Hurdles jumping through all the stakes
High pressure defines the greats
Carpe diem
Keep going watch those dreams
Flourish
Take a chance have the courage
Pursuit
Passion
Go out and make it happen

Go with your gut
We ignore the signs the feeling
Not having a pulse on where we are going
Decision to decision
Confused
Did I choose correctly?
But, we know the answer
Feel it in our bones
Ignoring it
Making wrong decisions trying to make it fit
Ultimately, we want to shift focus
Blame others making us feel at our lowest
When we all along were trying to be polite
But, creating our own plight
Not listening to our inner voice
Over here over here this is the right choice
Our gut always knows
No more need to lurk in the shadows
Listen to it, feed it
Even though it might not speak
Don't fight the feeling
You know intuition
Come on wake up listen
For admission
If not taken comes at it's cost
Admit to what you feel
As it is never wrong

Drive

You can always teach someone to drive
They have to jump behind the wheel
It's not knowledge that bridges the gap
It's the willingness to to make moves to cover the map
You can be guided
Real leaders stand, we decided
Not to be one-sided or divided
To move and make moves
We aren't a passenger
We are the carrier
Our messages and our words
Just sitting there is for the birds
That isn't for us
Active we must be
To help shape society
Complaints is just filling space
It's up to you to be the face
Each one of us makes decisions
Influences by messages on our televisions
Any screen
See we have more power
Than you think, so think of that energy you put out
Making a change in your direct life
Cut through your goals like a knife
Consistent
Persistent

Keep growing
It's your drive that keeps you going

<u>Room to grow</u>
Vacancy
Seems to be missing
Like a missing piece
Struggling to find peace
No where to go
Held at the bottom
The only way is up
To expand
Think grand
Mistakes are apart of the plan
To evolve
Grow
You never know
As you always have room to grow
To learn, to be, experience
Impact
With great tact
Anything you can comprehend is possible
Open your mind nothing's impossible
Room
Is just a space
Like your mind it can take you to any place

Goals

It is always great to have a benchmark
A place where regardless you see the light in the dark
Something you can measure
No matter the weather
Tinkering pulling twisting levers
To get to the goal
It takes self control
A place where you know it is achievable
Within reach and believable
Checking off your list
One by one as you persist
To be a goal digger
Making your aspirations and dreams even bigger
Keep going
Never knowing
Even when the result is within reach
It's attainable positive thoughts should always be in your internal speech
You got this
Keep it going
Around the corner is bliss
So keep glowing
Go onward
And
Lean into
Success

Dance

The art of movement
Inspires
Takes you to another place
Turn it up a dial
Bump up your song
Get lost in it for a while
All that matters is your smile
Moving around
Not caring what people are seeing
Because you're moving to the beat
Showing everyone the heat
Keep dancing on dreams
Do your thing

Vibes

Sometimes we don't notice
The vibes we send out
When bad vibes come we are ready to check out
But, that is when we should listen
To the info that is given
There is sorrow
Weak heartbeat in their words
Lost
They need guidance
Instead of good riddance
But, they don't realize what they are emitting

And how it's affecting others
Spreading like wildfire
Positive or negative
The choice is yours
Speak your vibe and attract your tribe
At any moment the wind can take shape and set your sail
Learn and grow even when you fail
See we listened to your pain
But it's time to go and do great things
Vibes
Good vibes only
Don't need to act still
Smile help others smile
We all have our moments to be there for someone for a while

It's within

Look around
What do you see
Pandora's box
Waiting
To be open
Waiting for you to tap into it
Your potential, sitting there, waiting
Why are you waiting
And what are you waiting for
It was always there so just go
Let it release
And you will see
It was within you
Just believe
Tap into your brilliance
Ups and downs you can do the distance
Inspire millions, billions, maybe even trillions
The key is persistence
Find your inner voice
Turn it up a dial is the only choice, make noise
To set free your creativity
Splashes of paint on a canvas
Take risks take chances
It's you
The artist finally revealed
Dreams realized and coming true

Passion

It's a fire
Blazing in your chest
Igniting creativity above all the rest
Nothing but heart
To do what speaks to your soul
Gluing you together making you whole
Without it lost
Keeping it at any cost
For this drive
Is the key in the ignition
You feel it in your intuition
Whispering your directions
Navigation, sensory collections
Piecing it, piece by piece
Not mattering slow or fast
To get to the destination
Called passion
Better fasten
The ride is lit

Relax

Sometimes we just need a little TLC
To reboot and see
That the whole picture is just as important as the small
Doesn't matter if you fall
You can get back up again
Be anything you want and make new friends
Take a moment just for you
Breath in and just relax
The moments you stressed about have past
Focusing on the past just keeps you in the past
Move on
Take it easy
Find a time to not be busy
Just for you
Alone
To refocus
Center
Yourself

Creation

Staring at a blank canvas
To be either intimidated or exited
I choose excitement
Like lightning striking the paintbrush
Vibrant with each stroke to create a diamond
It doesn't come easy
Taking time and taking shape
So many attempts and strikes to the canvas
In a panic this madness happens
Taking chances and the paint splashes
Feeling like this creation is the only thing on the planet
A mission to illustrate
A higher state
Concentrate
Making a creation
With no hesitation
Full force even through the frustration
Trying to stop is the temptation
Every stroke is your salvation
Being on a higher vibration
Illuminating nations
That is our affirmation
Through our eyes and hands touching souls
Freeing our minds from controls
That shift in our focus, you are on a roll
Shoot for the stars and your goals

Silence the inner and outer critics hating
Your art is illuminating
Inspiring
Exhilarating
Stimulating
Validating
Keep creating
Your creation is waiting

Friendships

True friends are ones you pick up just where you left off
Fill each other's words
And don't have to fit a mold
Because you can act young or old
Timeless
No time to expire
Even when you have struggles wishing for it to retire
You fight for each other
Caring for one another
Sometimes you don't get to hang often
Each time you hang out you bring out each other's awesome
The friendship blossoms
Evolving and revolving around all the fun
Creating memories to reminiscing
From beginning to forgiving
The ups and downs
Gone through it all
But together great friends are always there when you fall
A call, text, dm away
There to be a ear any day
Got your back when you need it
Keep it real when you need to hear it
Loyal to a fault
Locking your secrets like a vault
They are always there through it all
A friend you can rely on and call

Thanks for being a friend
Being there to the end
My ride or die
My butterfly
Firefly
Glows up my day I just can't deny
Each time our friendship soars in the sky
With a great friend like you I know I can take any leap and fly

Play

We get so busy with life we forget the grass
It was never just on the other side we just let it pass
Not noticing it was there all along
All we had to do was dig in and dance to a song
Mystical and at a distant it seems
Even if for a brief moment to laugh or have a gentle moment
Who are we deceiving
What are we achieving
By holding back our inner child to play
Dance in the rain
Laughter, joy, and smiles help break the chain
We each have moments to lighten a mood
Change the color of a tone in the room
Enabling our inner child to set free
Coloring the walls and everything we see
Just let loose and play
It may just change your whole day

New beginnings

Our past always seems to creep on us
Like a bad dream
They are there as reminders
Not to go back, but to look back
To break a cycle that should no longer be had
To build and create from scratch
Watch as a new beginnings will hatch
All lessons learned and still learning
Growing
Taking risks
Not knowing the final result
But embracing the new journey to indulge
In a fresh moment
Creating and paving a new path
No longer letting the past hold you back
Sometimes very difficult when the scars are dug deep
But, the new vibe takes shape and seeps
Into your heart beat
Making you slowly see the results you never imagined
If you never took that leap
You would never see the amazing possibilities
Everyday is a chance to a new beginning
Jump in
Hashtag #winning

The world in our hands

We sometimes feel like a small fish in a big pond
Or just a rook on a chess board
But, we are the universe to our minds
Removing the truth you will find
If you open your heart and ears
Listen and you will see
That the world is yours
You can be anything you want to be
It's all in your head
Yes there are steps
But, the choices are up to you
To stay true and believe in the process
Launching our ideas into space
To create
To be our thoughts and intentions
Manifesting takes our greatest attention
To ascension
Grow
You never know the impact
And who it will inspire
The next leaders to lead
The scientists who feed creativity
The world is at our fingertips
It's in our hands
Just all apart of God's plan
Time to expand

Enslaved

We let people and things hold a power
They hold us bound to their words
Instead of forming our own thoughts
We are born and taught
Listen to these voices they are suppose to lead
But, it seems they are leaders of greed
With the need
To control all around
Instead of representing the world we really need now
Rumbling sounds of one
Stand up
From one comes two
Noises increase
How do we make peace
When our people are left in the streets
Leaders are sirens
But no actions are met
To help pick up our fellow man
To give them a helping hand
What is man without the fruits of our land
And to share them with each other
Instead with a measuring cup we look at who's are filled
and who's are not filled up
Why can't we share
Where did we go to lose care

For the world is our thoughts and those are the fruits we bare
So here
One by one we can unbound each other
Help one another
Care for one another
Small steps to quantum
We can all march as one
Human Race
Not enslaved to the wires
Cutting ties from the web
Living in the moment uplifting each other
To live present
Not hand clasped to a phone
Perhaps a hand or hug
To help our wounds heal
And be real
Don't let our technologies steal
And rob you of living in the moment
No longer enslaved just go for it
Free
Run in the forest and trees
Be one with the wind
Each of us can help be the solution!

Rebirth

As you come to a close it is an opening for a new beginning
A new way of giving
To be still and enjoy the moment
To evolve
To create
To see a new life take shape
The old no longer serving
The new keeps growing
Skin shedding
Higher thoughts elevating
A new state
A rebirth
Taking place

Fearless

What you believe you become
Your thoughts transcend to your reality
When we live in fear
We are blocked and don't know how to live clear
Blurred
Scarred
Past holding us down
When breaking past it all will bring you to your inner crown
What you know you have inside
You keep hidden and want to hide
It slowly seeps out
But your held to fear of everything now
Afraid to speak up
Afraid to say what is on your mind
Afraid to be judged
Afraid you are judging yourself
Afraid of what others perceive
Afraid to be yourself
Where is the freedom
When chaos is crawling all over your mind
Holding you back from what you are meant to be
To run wild and free
Releasing your creativity
Knowing and doing anything you put your mind to
Be you

Fearless from all that is holding you back
Who cares how others react
As now you can finally be
Yourself
You hold the power
It's all in your head
You can do it if you think you can
You can't if you think you can't
To become fearless
You must look deep into fears face
And say you don't belong in my heart my chest get out of this place
No longer scared
Comfort in the uncomfortable
Pioneering a new fate
No longer being controlled by perceptions
Fearless inception
Running toward fear not away
As it no longer has room in your head to play
Anything is possible
Endless nothing impossible
Keep growing, trying, and showing
The only barrier is all in our mind
Get to it, rid your fears, and you will shine
Fierce fearlessness
Fearlessly free
Just to be

Patience

Irony
Always rushing for a result
Blaming never taking fault
O-well I was in a rush
Making such a fuss
Didn't realize the self sabotage
Not embracing a single moment
Not knowing
I was out of flow
Because of the cycle I kept keeping
Toxins kept creeping
I couldn't just wait
Let the ideas grow
I wanted to rush to the destination
Becoming destination unknown
Instead of embracing the journey
Mind clouded feeling dirty
If I just would of waited
Not hesitating
Using my instinct
But letting it grow
Organic
Not problematic
For taking your time
To see the whole rhyme
The picture

Not a glimpse
Getting out of my head mind tricks
Taking it step by step
Observing the moment
Embracing it and holding it
Taking my time to see the whole pie
Deciphering through lies
As if I should use my intuition
And be patient
I would of seen what was needed
I stopped rushing to a destination
Now just open my eyes to each with freedom of expression
As patience does not come easy
But is simple
You must let the picture be drawn
Never rushing to a conclusion
Patience is a ingredient that always makes your recipe right
As it takes time to cook and ignite
Practicing the virtue of pacing
Not racing
Not rushing
But absorbing
Not ignoring
Pause
Take a breath
Let it breathe

Patience is the key
In unlocking your destiny
Keep pushing toward goals
Not everyday do we feel efficient
Sometimes not worthy or sufficient
There are lessons in each hurdle
Even if the pace feels like your moving like a turtle
Each experience shapes who you are
And what you are about to become
Keep striving
Keep driving
Keep going
Keep motivated
Use your drive
And thrive
To your goal
It is always worth it
Even when you have to dig yourself out of a hole
Because that goal is meant to be met
By destiny and relentless action
Yourself is the true bet
So all cards in
Keep working

Last shot

If you only had one more shot
How would you reinvent yourself to be hot
Not for the gram or the likes
But removing jealousy to build your legacy
We all live like we have several shots
Not realizing each moment is your one and only shot
Because once that moment passes it is gone forever
There is no restart button
Living like we will live forever
This isn't Tuck Everlasting
This is real life
Your moment is in every simple decision cutting like a knife
Irreversible
Deep ingrained
Shaping everything
What if you started taking every moment as your last shot
Making a slam dunk
Not caring about the haves and the have-nots
Because you are measuring up to your own ways
Leading the pack with your wordplay
Because it's your words to your actions
The only way to get satisfaction
Is to let each shot count
Each moment now
We don't have twenty lives just one

Every breath could be your last
So why don't you live a little
Give a little
Be bigger than your imagination
As today is your last shot
Go ahead and take it
Make it swish
If you don't there is always another shot to rebound
Just don't ever quit!

Human vs. Machine

Inspired by Elon Musk

Interesting what we see and perceive
It's our consciousness and what we believe
Something that machines can't conceive
Because they don't have a pulse
No heart
They are given commands
But, what about humans
What makes us different
Is it inherent
Or are we apart of natural selection
Selecting, generation to generation
The evolution of humanity
Technology tracking us I find is inhumanity
But, we are letting it take over
We got too comfortable with the trust of technology
Which will soon play us like monopoly
If we don't wake soon to the data we are giving
Our footprint may no longer exist
Imagine wires as veins
No longer a pulse beating
The verge of destruction
Was our self-illusion to overshare
Soon it will be used against us feeling like a nightmare
Humans versus our own creation

Irony is we started this fixation
To lead man to the most intelligent
But, while creating we have been so negligent
The fact is our data will be used against us
Or has it already is the question
Election to what you see on your newsfeed selected
We have been trusting our computers for a century
But, there will be a point that we will be obsolete, rudimentary
Our intelligence versus what we made that will be far superior it will dominate
Wipeout and eliminate
If we don't safeguard our future
Humanity will be no longer
Just binary code
Data that will implode
We feel while data and facts don't
It's our next decisions that hold
It's literally in our hands
Double take when you glance at your phone
Shocking I know
It starts here now
System overload
It's heavy, but it's better to see it coming then to be shocked
Only we can construct
Instruct our future

Humanity
A bloodline
Not wires and fake news
A real pulse
It involves all of us
To be more discerning
Safeguards and conserving
Our minds and our data
Our feeling and our race
The human race

Heal

All I want is to put my hands on you
Make you feel all wounds disappear
No more sorrows, no more pain, no more fears
Your pain makes me sad
I want to just make it all better, but I can't
It's not in my hands as I thought it was
It is in the vibrations I send out to you
Do you feel them working there way to you
Cloaking your whole being making you feel everything
Finally free from the hurt and pain
That was once driving you insane
Now no longer
Crazy right
Your suddenly feeling stronger
Negative thoughts game over
Your positive thoughts taking over
You start to realize
And recognize your strength
It hasn't been easy
When the pain hits making you feel uneasy
But, now you got me
I'm by your side regardless
Helping you heal through all the hardship
The alpha omega artist
Striking cords making pure music
To sonically change your mood

Lifting to a freeing altitude
As your sorrow no longer exists
Just happiness
To smile once again
Laugh all over again
For the pain has gone
A new good vibe has caught on
Healing
Your whole body
Head to toe
Finally, not feeling prisoner
And knowing where you must go
Go to goals
And score
There is no more room for anguish anymore
As you are healing
No longer a cut
Just a scar to remind you where you traveled
Represents the battles
But, your heart is free finally to unravel
No more fear
You see and feel clear
As you can finally listen and hear
There is no more pain for you to bear
For I am here
Helping you heal
The change feeling unreal

The magic inside higher and higher you feel
A mindset you can finally go and be fierce
As the past and the old no longer serve what you feel in your heart
Healing is the restart
Time to reboot
This is just the beginning the prelude

There is always time

Sometimes it seems hopeless
Limited
But it is in the factor that we don't expand our minds
There is always time
Just don't let the time run out from your dreams
It's not la la land it's the real thing
You can make it happen just keep working

Depression

Inspired by Stevie Wonder

It's not a funny moment it is a low moment
That has us held
Deconstructing all we have built
Making us feel less than worth it
Beyond worthless
At a all time low
Feeling like we are drowning with no where to go
Is it our past
Is it our environment
Is it the neurons in our brain
Is it the struggle and pain
We feel lost in the sea
Blind to anything happy
Numb
Feeling less than one
Not one hundred percent
Trapped in bed
Trying to avoid everything
Not wanting to be around anyone or anything
Thinking to oneself is this natural
Or habitual
Why do I get so stuck
I want to move on but there are triggers that suck, the mere energy out of me

What happened
It was a past moment holding our future moments back
Letting us not feel whole just feeling cracked
But we need to snap out of all of that
Depression
It's toxic and takes over
Feeling sorry for ourselves is not the cure
Staying in bed avoiding everything isn't pure
We must get out and experience the world
Take a breath in and speak to our friends
Share our pain so we can release our toxins that keep self sabotaging you
For depression never belongs inside of you
You are more than enough
Surround yourself with those who bring the best out of you and you will see
That mere feeling was never meant to be
You are alive and free
No more tears and hiding
You can be the hero of your own story
Stop drowning in the sorrow and fight against those voices
That run around like ants in your head
Making you feel less
People who make you feel less remove them
They don't belong in your orbit
You are scared but a champion of life
So get out of that depression you are a ray shining bright

Never dim down for those who don't appreciate you
Can't see the value you bring
You are loved and here to sing
You belong just right here
Stop letting others judgments of you hold you back from being the real you
It's okay to be out in a low but know it's temporary because you never know the amazing moment waiting around the corner
That will change your whole life for the better
It might be that life-changing moment you never believed could happen
Miraculous things can happen
So I know it's hard but make the shift
Accept the pain, but triumph and sing in the rain
For our struggles make everything worth it
That's where diamonds are made
The is no time for your head to be down
There is a whole world waiting for you to show up right now

Synchronicity

Like a puzzle and the pieces seem to fit right in
Everything aligning
It's amazement, can't even believe it is happening
Magic
Seeming to see all the connections
Lining up all the dots and seeing the full picture
Life expanding getting richer and richer
As the roots dig deeper and deeper into the soil
And the branches grow
You see the connectivity
Everything in synchronicity
Wires and vibrations all connected
Feeling the magic of signs being directed
Guided to your greatness
Take a leap come on be courageous
As you have the confirmation
Keep growing into that blossoming celebration
For every moment is in sync
You just have to believe
Take a moment and you will see
You can become anything you conceive
Look at all the interweaving and interconnecting on your path
You were made to bask
In your talent
Let it beam

Ripping at the seams to gleam
Aligning everything
It isn't just serendipity
It's complete synchronicity
Moving like a river
Moving fast getting bigger and bigger
All events deriving purpose
Removing your fear no longer getting nervous
For it all makes sense
It matches up if you just took a outsiders look
You would see everything from the present to what it took
It is all coming together
To this one moment
Now
Present
Manifesting from your mind to the people you have beside
You created it fully in sync
So open your mind
It's all in what you believe
You can set forth and achieve
Anything
You are your own synchronicity

Originality

All art evolves from influences
Pure creativity
Making a honest source of originality
Not a copycat
But a influence
Those who copy are not original
As they don't find there own identity
Ready to mirror others creativity
Instead of using it and taking it to imagination
Art encourages each other to push the boundaries of our minds
Creating storms of ideas like fast running turbines
Influencing fresher ideas
Not stealing, but making an imprint
For copycats have a fear to free their own mind
They are creatively blind
Because they can't strike their own ideas
A real originator is influenced, but creates their own masterpiece
Masterfully
Giving a new look at something you never thought of
Because truth be told almost everything has been done
It's nice to see originality
Refreshing
For being unique is the key
No need to ever copy

Just be you and I'll just be me
Mastermind of creativity
The OG of originality

Happiness

It is just waiting
Waiting to seep out
Laughter and smiles that can't contain themselves
For your imagination is open
Possibilities flowing
Being true to you
Exploring the fun
You once lost
By repressing all your thoughts
Now you only think of shining moments
That spread from what you are knowing
You are great
You are everything you imagined and more
The cup overflowing as you are ready to explore
That deep need inside of who you need to be
The treasure lying inside, keep digging
As it brings you pure joy
Jubilee
For you are no longer blocked and can see
You set your mind free from negativity
And only hold positivity
Making only smiles breach
As the things holding you back you had to unteach
They were not serving you
To lead you to your center
Of where you can radiate

All negativity around you, you now have to eliminate
The key is your surroundings, you need to regulate
You have the choice in where, who, and in what you participate
Partake in the happy
Not in those that make you feel crappy
Bring you to a low
For when you are low you feel trapped with nowhere to go
Orbiting on the downright negative
Instead of taking off to outer space
And keeping a positive outlook and outtake
For your happiness is important
Do what you love
Don't ignore it
You deserve to be happy
Don't let someone crabby not on your frequency make you feel badly
For you should gladly elevate, and keep it classy
Stay unbothered
Why bother
For your happy is deserved
Don't let that outer world get you unnerved
Their goal is to get you disturbed
As they are not in there happy place
So observe take note and go to your own healthy space
Whether boundaries are needed or not
Your happiness deserves to be fought

A smile on your face
A overjoyed feeling all over your body, you are ready to embrace
You deserve to be happy
So smile let it sink in for this is not a race
It's just you, and you, and you needing to conserve your sacred space
To be everything you imagined and more
Happiness is knocking at your door
Open and let it spread
For the old you has just shed

Focus

Distractions
Playing all around us
Trying to skew and navigate us
When you keep circling around your soul
Ignorant to the whispers taking a toll
As our heart keeps showing us what we need
But, we keep up with all these socials, texts, and newsfeeds that are so distracting
Can't maintain what I need
Lost focus
All these things orbiting shifting my attention, feeling hopeless
So much noise in my mind and around causing tension
Feeling paralyzed because everything is pulling me in multiple directions
Entering several dimensions
Losing myself as I try to keep up
Feeling like my head is spinning
Too much I have put on my plate
Realizing I need to re-navigate
Calibrate
For the mind in pure nature can only do one thing at a time
To pour my focus as this shift can take place anytime
Focus, focus, focus
It's the magical potion
Hocus Pocus

It's how you become spellbound to execution
To complete what you set out
No longer subject to all the shiny commotion
You have complete utter focus
The task at hand
Not caring if anyone understands
Because you know what it takes
Go out there give it your all
Watch as you see with your focus all the pieces align and fall
Right into place
Focus is that happy place
Determined
For one thing at a time will get you everything you need
Maintain focus and you will get there
Distractions beware
Because they no longer belong here
Step by step
Moment by moment
It's the focus you need that is growing
Exponential
Mind laser focused
Focus, focus, focus
When you do the results will be explosive

Freedom

By design we are meant to be free
Nothing holding you back just pure energy
Not held by suggestion
Trusting your inner guide and intuition
For the fact and truth is we all bleed
Humans programmed for greed
When the true need has to be freed
It is about humanity
Not a monopoly
Love, real love, honestly
Compassion
Absorbing each other's unique voice
Our self freedom is a choice
And for those who are not free
It's our voices coming together to set them free
For those oppressed are not able to see
Blinded by the roots programmed in there minds
Desensitized to mankind
Because those who oppress are hurt using more hurt
There is no solution in pain
What is to gain
When one is not free
And held in captivity
For our freedom came at a price
Through the struggle what happened wasn't right
But, history we must let remain as a lesson of past

So stereotypes we can blast
They don't serve
No culture deserves
Rotten stigmas
Need to be replaced
For the future is to be embraced
Where we are all free from the stigmas that put a hold on society
Freedom as it rings in
Open world the answers start within
Each of our actions
Freedom is a chain reaction
Fight the stigmas
And we will see an ocean of possibly
Waves of courage and exploring curiosity
For our cultures and colors rain great opportunity
Universally
Connected
Freedom is the gate to heaven
Walk on the clouds
Float in the sea
Our free starts with you and me
Everybody
Imagine the possibilities

Transformation

People say they want to change
But, they want it in a instant
It doesn't happen overnight so they are hesitant
For change that happens on a deeper level
Only occurs over time
But, they want life like their newsfeed and timeline
Post and poof, I have changed
That is not the case
For a caterpillar to fly
Has to be sheltered in it's cocoon to eventually blossom out and fly
So why do we want to fly when we haven't constructed our wings
Who programmed us to think that we can just jump and do all these things
It's several moments that build for us to leap and have our wings
Ready to fly
It just doesn't happen when you snap two fingers
It figures
We all are striving to be winners
First place
But, how can you be in a race when you are not ready
Preparation is key
Several actions that create the sum of one
To keep your focus, laser-focused like a gun

To hit your target and never miss
Day in and out
Transformation hits
For the slight change that you make to your day
Everyday creates that moment to fly
You are building through so breathe in the journey as it is
time to blossom butterfly
Go ahead and fly

Impact

Everyone has a voice
We all have a choice
To make great change
To impact everything
By just each of our actions
One at a time shifting directions
Navigating not only our ship but others
So truth be told just be a blessing unto others
For the beauty is in our cultures
It is sharing and living our vibrant colors
To have impact
Simple from smiles, hugs, to eye contact
Only add value not subtract
Hold brace as turbulence may occur, but the growth is
opulent in this growth spurt
For direct change is inevitable
You voice making change in this world is incredible
Living your purpose intentional
Fighting against the conventional
For being unique is delectable
For your story is impactful
Share, open up, and care
For your purpose is to be right here
Be the impact you wish to see
Your voice illuminating
With your strength

Warm embrace
Inspiring the human race
To evolve
Problem solve
For we all need to our world to revolve around each other and get involved
Together global consciousness and thoughtfulness is where we can get all our problems solved
That is how we make the greatest impact

Simplicity

Funny that we make moments full of complexities
Giving ourselves great anxieties
When the easiest way is to keep it simple
Simplicity is letting the ease twinkle
For complicated only exists
When you create all these tangles and twists
Keep it straightforward
Easy, and you will move onward
Simple is the best adventure
All Aboard
For it's time to ease in and explore
It isn't complicated
That is appreciated
Everyone can understand
And connect
The complex we have to reject
Kiss kiss
Keep it simply simple
Simplicity

Consistency

Being in a flow state
There is no way to hesitate
As one foot passes the other
Goals after goals synchronized with one another
It all starts and ends with small moves
You have nothing to prove
As consistency is the magic that gets you through
Step by step guiding the way
For nothing will blossom without a consistent change
Keep it up
Consistency will get you higher up
To that unimaginable sight
Higher and higher in height
Into the clouds and your dreams
Consistency is the truth
So pursue it by all means
It will take you exactly to your destination every time
It's no secret just takes time
Build and be brilliant
It's all about being consistent

Beauty

We are always looking at the outside
When beauty resonates from the inside out
Inner is just as important
As the outer
Working as an orchestra
To create the perfect Picasso
For beauty is not just the makeup painted on ones face
It is the aura the energy someone provides in a space
It radiates
You can tell confidence
And the power it brings
For your beauty always sings
It begins with the initial note
That starts with your soul
The heart and passion you bring never getting old
For our age is a number and beauty on the exterior fades
The perfect beauty inside never leaves
For our definition of beauty deceives
It is really what you give and receive
We are all energy
Moving around
It's not about wearing the finest tux or gown
It's the heart inside
The true beauty you can't hide
For the shell you can dress up
But, a real heart you can always tell

The beauty illuminating
For your beauty starts within
And shines out
Be beautiful the journey always starts from the inside out
When you walk by the energy shifts putting jaws to the ground
As everyone says WOW

Serendipity

Winds are moving while storms come and go
There is magic in the air
Leading you beyond imaginable
For the notes in the sky
Playing your favorite song
Bring you and others to enjoy along
There are strange events that bring people together
Seeming like a miracle
When no matter what the outcome will align
In due time
Hearts
Beating
Surfaces heating
As one event to another seem like magic
Out of the blue it just happens
These serendipitous moments that take your breath away
As if it was written out word for word in a screenplay
That moment you lift your head up at a cafe
And reconnect
Or meet a stranger
Realizing they will no longer be a stranger
For you have connected it's a life and game changer
The universe is like Rembrandt a painter
Putting together events and people
Seeing humanity as it should we are all equal
Serendipity plays it's role

It is just so mystical
As it all aligns and comes together
The saying we know so well
Birds of a feather
Forming
Becoming a force unexplainable
For there is magic in what happens
And how it happens
Energy to atoms
This is all a balance
Equation
Being constantly written
As serendipity plays
The conscious it raises
As it makes sense for you paving a path to blaze
Bring forces together to be explosive
Serendipity
It's just your luck
A life of good fortune!

Secrets

It's funny we try to hide it
But the truth always seeps out
Whispering secrets
To the wind brushing upon truth
It knocks on your door
Or knocks you on the floor
We think a secret can hide forever
But, it always comes to the surface
For air it breathes
As there is always truth beneath
Running away trying to hide these secrets
Locking it in a safe as you thought it was a safe place
But, the key seems to pop up randomly as a sign
Held and released at the inopportune time
Making us turn shades of red we never imagined
Scared to share our passions
Not saying a word and taking no action
Hiding from our truth is tragic
For the fear of being revealed, it just happened
But, it's the true you and your gifts you have concealed
For the raw and authentic self
You locked away
Hiding, until one day
Forces of nature took course
Revealed your secrets galloping on a dark horse
Expelling all you thought you were

To what you really are
No more secrets
For you finally accept your uniqueness
The special you no more secrets
For it's your truth finally speaking

Motivations

Is it a goal
Is it instinct
Is it a desire
Is it an angel
Is it an inner fire
Blazing a new trail
Keeping your consistency to prevail
As sweat, tears, and hard work are put in
That inner flame driving you keeping you motivated
For you have a vision you must see through
Not everyone understands you
Mystified by your being
Not understanding
But, you know your motivations so keep going
Even when your on the brink of stopping
It's your inspiration that keeps you wanting
That need to get to the end
To complete what you have set forth
Even when sometimes you feel lost
Or like a ghost
And no one notices
Your patience and persistence
Always reveals your efforts with no interference
It is not easy to stay on course
So easy to be thrown off course
But, it is the end vision the result

Small moves by small moves that help you catapult
Into something you never imagined
All possibilities happening
For your motivation
Was guided by your inspiration
Which leads to amazing creations
That created a cycle of unbelievable things
No one imagined the boundaries and magic to what was happening
It was all in your vision to see it through
You never know what amazing things you can do
Keep going
Never knowing
How close the result is
For motivation
Keeps your engine going
Stay motivated
Inspire the world with your art
And you will see all the magic start
Reignite your motivation
As imagination aligns information
As greatness within is your affirmations
No explanation
Gives your soul liberation
What gave you your purpose and drive
For you are alive
To strive and thrive

From your inspirations to flame your motivations
Put the work in your just getting started

Value

Money
Power
Respect
Integrity
Loyalty
Truth
All are values on a scale
As the wind moves in several directions on the sails
For we understand there are levels to this game called life
Trying to provide
To our friends, family, and ourselves
Sometimes we lose track of what's most important
Things become unbalanced and some areas outweigh the others
Losing care for one another
Lost our value and others around
Trying to pick ourselves back up from the ground
Shattered
Mattered
For balance is key
Everyone's balance is so different you see
It's figuring out your value and what you bring
Your purpose is the plug for everything
The only way to elevate your value
Is to move out of the shallow
And refocus, don't get stuck in the vacuum

For you have worth
See your value is the rebirth
As time keeps ticking
Your value will resonate and you will be winning
Everything you touch is your essence
A gift from the heavens
Acknowledge the value you bring
You are here to make the angels sing
There is no price tag on your value
Priceless
For your mindset has been heightened
Valuable as can be
Only a viewpoint from struggles and learning is victory
They are building blocks to a profound future
For you are the writer, creator, & producer
Anything is possible when you see your value in the mirror
Abundance and love growing bigger and bigger
As you have removed all fear to see your worth
Now go out there and get to work!

Lucky luck

The wind hits
And you feel it on your cheeks
And you know today is going to be one of the luckiest days ever
So never say never
As luck is waiting in the corner
Ready to burst so don't be a hoarder
Share the wealth you are about to get
Cause your luck can spread
All great things on their way then
So smile and embrace the fun
As your luck has just begun
Lucky you
Three wishes
Anything can happen
Magic
Your shock will be funny to caption
But finally great things to share
For your luck is here
Here to stay and rub off on everything
Destiny
Seems so predictable
But, life is so unpredictable
There is no roadmap
Even when you think there is navigation
Sometimes it's our own will and with no explanation

We have no idea where it is going
Just a feeling of knowing
Your making the right decision
Truth is all decisions are right
We forget the light in learning in the dark
We are smart
But, it's not predictable
Indescribable
A force we can't explain
For it sometimes feels like a mind game
It just feels right like when Cinderella gets her glass slipper
Destined
For a higher worth
For it's our love and passion
That drives us even when we don't know the destination
For destiny is awaiting
Without hesitation
Keep making decisions
For everything aligns use your intuition
Destiny is the equation it will always be no matter the variables
So keep striving to be the best version of you that you can be
Your legendary destiny
As you gain clarity to make a legacy

Never say never

Expression or a saying
Never say never
Seen on a yacht
Seeming impossible to be bought
But, there it is floating in the ocean as the sun is peaking to say welcome
For never is yet not impossible
Everything is probable
So instead of spending time doubting everything
Start believing and you will see anything
Anything can happen and will
It's all in your mind
Flip the switch on
You are about to get on
You can never believe from an idea to what you can conceive
Never say never
It's your time to believe
Anything is possible just set your mind and achieve
Watch your wildest dreams as they are seen
Never say never
It's ironically clever
As possibilities are eternal
As you grow with purpose
Learning to show more love and connecting is universal
Next time you hear

Never say never
Smile and see vast possibilities
As they approach your future igniting creativity

Leadership

One with a finite mind
May never expand their world
For leadership is to be expansive on ideas
Not to limit there flow
But, to provide the soil to assist in their growth
A leader is born and made
For they carry the world as a renegade
Thinking different is there trade
Seeing images of a world that needs to be
And then creating it
No dictatorship
Partnerships
A mutual vision
To rise to the higher good
Even in times of being misunderstood
They rise above showing what it takes to lead
It is not all easy you see
There can be controversy
But, they handle it with gentle care and grace
Even compose themselves when it gets heated
For all mistakes
Are lessons that it takes
To lead it takes patience
To be great
Hurdles to show strength
And a mindset to win

Against all odds a true leader prevails
From their community
For they built this for them
It was never about the leader
They are sent as God's teacher
Not a preacher
A guide to light up there surroundings
That's what a leader should be
Just the one to ignite flames inside hearts hiding
For our passion strikes and lights a path unimaginable
Leaders and leadership is finding the strength to compose greatness in every step
For each action has a reaction
And every word holds power
A leaders message provides warm on hearts
Brings unity
As we all may have differences
But, when you take out a heart literally there is no difference
Humanity at its pure
A gift
With no ego
Real leaders defined to fight those with no voice
That have no choice
Each of us inside have the ability
It's within us to practice humility
Moments of compassion and kindness

Seeing all truths removing the blindness
For each of us lies a leader in our community
It's time for us to lead the peace

Instinct

Just an animal in the wild
Our primitive thoughts and desires
Ignite fires
Rain emotions
As the world is a jungle of noise
Feeling surrounded
Trapped by thoughts
Realizing they are distracting us
From listening to what we feel
Trying to sort fake from real
Understanding the hunt
For we are either predator or prey
Awaiting our fate
Or jumping in and doing what it takes
We listen to the wind and the sounds around
Quietly moving tiptoeing around
Gently absorbing the environment
You meet
You see
You listen
You feel
It's all within in you in that instant
Your instinct
The whispers in your gut
Either you listen or undercut
For it always speaks

Listen, it really knows and speaks
It can tell you the truth as it never lies
Hides words as disguise
As it is a pure feeling
That speaks
Fight or flight
Take the high road you just might
Your body is telling you all you need to know
Your mind is conflicting you on where to go
The decision must be made
What will you listen to
Instinct or words coming out
I believe the vibe tells all
Listen to your instinct

Recalibrate

Moments of silence
To be still
Tranquil
Refreshing
A new breath
To finally take
The magic it will make
To restart
No more frustrations
A stroke of luck
Striking at the stroke of midnight
The courage to start breeds light
For your heart inspires and ignites
Anew
Reinvigorating it feels
The ease of change
As all you needed
Was a moment to recalibrate
Be brave
That moment is for you
To dig deep and fight for what's best for you

Resilience

Inspired by Lola

We have the pain and feeling of giving up
But, it's these whispers you are strong enough
Worth it
Keep fighting
Get back up
That help guide you to stand up and keep going
As you are finally flowing
Adrenaline
Action
Greatness is your manifestation
For resilience is in your blood
It's the words you speak into your mind
Your hustle and grind
Your light you illuminate to help not only yourself but, others shine
It's not always easy
Hardship are hurdles
You jump over
For you are a champion
Ready no matter the outsides reaction
You were built for this
Wipe off that sweat and keep going
Your beauty is in your resilience
Persistence

It's all in you
For it becomes what you do
How you react
Keeping your mind intact
For every battle is a victory
Lessons learned and challenges met
Glorious
To win the race
You must win in your mind
For it determines your effort and belief
Whispers of greatness and goodness to achieve
Anything possible
Nothing impossible
For your tact is all measured by your resilience to face any challenge
Challenge accepted
It's your beliefs and thoughts that keep you directed
Go and choose your direction
For the mirror is just a reflection
What do you see
How do you feel
Resilient
Keep going
The battle of great thoughts
It's all in your mind
It is what you believe
New perspectives

Surprise
It's a new viewpoint
A way to see different than before
It is invigorating to explore
Opens yourself to a whole new whole new world
A new language
Seeing different angles
A several vantage points collide
To listen and hear from embrace the ride
It's refreshing to be in a element where you can just learn
Learning is something we just yearn
To keep seeing new places, spaces, and technologies
It's crazy when they end up going back in time to study our anthropology
It is the changes that make evolution so interesting

New perspectives

Ignite change in the air
Some lost gasping for air
Others adapting with no despair
For change is great
Pioneers
Reaching higher levels creating newer mountains to climb
and achieve
For these new ways are the waves of the future
There is no doubt then to just believe
Here to stay
It will be the New Way
Newer perspectives to elevate
Thought
Mind
Money
Intelligence
Humanity
Spark
Visions
The lense that ignited a path to lead
For we are inspired
Focus on passions and drive is what we need
To keep the fire alive inside
Not to hide
To shine so bright
For it's that initial spark

That lit up the dark
That whispered to your heart
That got you to jump on and start
For the beginning is just your opening
And the leap of faith just knowing
It will all happen
The magic within hearing noises of clapping
Bringing unity to our hearts
For we all wanted the same thing
Just a little spark
Miracles that make your mark
Spark, Spark, Spark

Reinvent

Wisdom in our words
Actions said
But, there is always time to reinvent
The page is blank
Ready to be rewritten

Confidence

A person of valor
Is one who is knocked down
But, keeps getting back up
It's stamina, strength, drive, and confidence
Many struggle with illusions of it
Instead of stepping into it
It is a battle
Internal thoughts rattle
As you absorb an abundance of emotions
Trying to understand the commotion
Not realizing our own behaviors was the perpetrator
Composing melodies of "jaws"
Da da da da duh da
The suspense of our blurred mind
Jarring us from action
Self sabotaged satisfaction
Every ten steps forward taking twenty back
Not understanding it was our confidence we lacked
Slowly shining a mirror to the discovery
How cruel could we have been to the image we have seen
Denying the greatness in the mirror
You are the universe
You are your own superhero
If you could only see the powers within
And not give in
To the false identity that judgements prescribed

By having confidence in who you are
And blessed you are alive
Each day is a blessing and a lesson
To live the most confident life
Soak in this confidence
You are alive
Riveting
Breathing
Moving
Shining
Your beauty no longer has to hide
Be confident for there is only one you
Perfectly imperfect in all it's glory
Strut your worth
With all your words
It works from the inside out
You will feel it when it radiates out
Confidence
You are born to be a queen or king
Ruler of your universe
Time to conqueror your mind
Positive thoughts rule
With only positive vibes
Screaming for your to put your own flavor
Not needing any approval, but your own
Reminder your are the one and only that owns your thrown
So slay, slay, slay

Today is your day
Rock out who you are everyday
No hesitations just time for you to play
And be released, finally free
Confident and fearless
Just a rockstar where we are all just a witness
Time to rock out being you!

Desires

Setting fire
To a desire
Watching it blaze
As it writes it's own page
It all takes a ton of work
Sacrifices
People skewing your perspectives
Getting you on and off path
Trying to fan out your flame
Because they don't understand
It's a inside game
Listening to everyone else is a detour, mind-game
Tricks crawling around in your brain
Not speaking to your heart
I can't remember, brain fart
Distracting you from the purpose of your start
Only you hold your desire
Only you can make it take fire
And blaze your own trail
So why let everyone judge
That is an easy way to guarantee of a fail
You have to believe so deep and have that desire
As the outside world is ruthless to put our your fire
So keep going
You know the reason
You don't have to defend or give any reason

Today it is your desires season
Keep lighting it up
Never giving up
For your desire
Can also spark someone's fire
And watch as it spreads
Real truth and bravery
Removing mind slavery
For we all have misconceptions
To fit in everyone's box
It makes us get lost in everyone else's thoughts
When what matters is what we think
That is when we can be free
To desire and dream

Legacy

Legends are born and created
But, legacy lasts a lifetime
Something that is past from generation to generation
Traditions and methods with no explanation
Just a way to put an imprint on all nations
Mentalities and realities
Subjective to all sorts of thoughts
Legacy isn't something that can be brought
For it is a societal right of passage
Legends chosen for the gifts and same with legacy
A person who provides a lifetime of greatness that leads to the evolution
It's a greatness revolution
Being passed down
Imprinting greatness on everyone
For the choice is not hard
It's to believe in your gifts as they will take you far
Legacy is something that will infinitely be remembered
And even when a legend is gone the legacy of their gifts always live on
It must be past down from generation to generation
To inspire the future leaders without explanation
Legacy is what we all strive to leave
Look in every small action what you can and will achieve
Your greatness is all in what you believe
It's not a miracle, it is you

Take action in what you do
Just watch the magic take over you
Your legacy will live on years beyond your existence
Maybe you will start seeing every action has significance
Grow, learn, bless, and be abundance with persistence
For true legends legacies never die they turn hearts on fire igniting missions
To love more than imagined to blaze passions and ambitions
Notice what lasts are traditions
Even in all conditions
A legacy lives on
Even when people don't realize where it came from
It Breathes
Impacting lives in so many ways
Consciousness raises
As it makes an imprint on our brains
Legacy or legend
It's all in your hands for you are the one who is destined
For progression
Leaves an impression
From your creative expressions
Painting your masterpiece
Watch as your tranquility and peace grows to increase
And the negatives decrease and you release
Your legacy

Vibrations

A vibe always introduces you, before you say hi
Your energy is either welcomed or unwelcome
It's a vibe
Vibrations create a space to be creative or be destructive
The energy chooses whether this person you met should be trusted
Without a word exiting their mouth
You start to wonder how
Is it intuition or instinct
But, it's pure energy so distinct
It made you feel before your brain could even formulate a thought
It's something we are born with it's not taught
Vibrations are sent out constantly
So if your not giving the right vibe
You have to figure out why
The source so you can readjust and get back on course
For vibe always attracts your tribe
Remember it's the vibe you give is the vibe that comes back to you
Radiate brightness and happiness
And it will always come back
Take in the hurdles and be cautious on how you react
Your vibration without explanation is your signature
So remember how you stamp your presence
Good vibes only

Magnetic

Forces pulling you
Directing your directions
Guiding conversations
To heavenly connections
Without a word escaping your mouth
These pulls are attracting you right exactly to the spot you need to be
Similar to serendipity
But, pulls igniting passions and burning desires
For inspirations have caught fire
As these pulls bring you to the place where you feel at home
A momentum in a new frequency zone
Flowing
Rivers and lava
Smoldering
Warming your heart
Magnetized no way to depart
As the powers are bringing exactly where you need to be
And who you need to meet
Even a struggle or lesson isn't defeat
It is a test whether you can stay on your feet
Magnetic
Pulls
You
Closer

To your desires
No
Stopping
Once it takes fire
No coincidences
A force unexplained
Just destined
Magnets attracting
You are everything

Enlightened people

A collective
A way of thought
Deeply rooted in opening worlds to a higher energy
A power so deep in our veins
It is no longer asleep
As one touches another one
Communicating metaphysically
Awakening with greetings
Spiritual Beings
All bleeding the same
For our shell is just to be protective
It's our inside that is so precious
Our heart and thoughts
Creating waves in the world
Making peace
Connecting all
To realize we are one
Together
Uniting all walks of life
Hearts beating all right on time
Cloaked energy
Bringing past, present, and future together
Living time travelers
Being enlightened
Touched
Deep glows in your eyes

Seeing your diamond shine
Exactly we all can be shining
When we finally take away the blind
Open our eyes
Raw real with no disguise
Our truth enlightens the world
To their truth
Make sure you are real and the real truth always prevails
Feel the energy transporting you to become your higher being
Enlightenment, a supreme feeling

Finding what you need

It's all around you
Surrounding
Making ripple effects and echoes to see whether you are listening
Hearts beating
Sounds seeping
Trying to ignore it
It will keep running into you
Like a re-recurring dream
Every time you try to escape
Signals come in circling your landscape
It's ironic it keeps you thinking
About all the time that has come and past
Just in a instant moment it could beat every dream you ever forecast
For what you need is now
This moment so make it last
Forget the past
In the now
A time traveler finally found
Supersonic rockstar
Underground hypnotic mobster
Living for and in that NOW

Falling in

I am on the verge of disaster or destiny
Removing all my force fields
Allowing you in
As I'm falling falling
So deep deep with you
No one else
I usually don't ever do this
But, I can see your heart and mine beating
Stargazing as they align
Running in the sand loosing time
Your touch makes me lose my mind
As I fall more in
Learning about you
Makes me feel whole
That missing piece I was missing
All this life you are giving
Euphoric
Two explorers
Exploring
Every ounce of your body
Your smile and your energy
Contagious
Injecting every beat in my heart
New beginnings and starts
Falling in

Rejection

In a form of a letter, call, text, or DM
Rejection happens
It is redirection magic
The path you thought it should of been was not a guarantee
Feeling strangely
Even when it stuck so deep in your mind and heart
It's telling you to reevaluate and restart
Not pause or freeze
Not be paralyzed
Not get nasty or mean
It's to look at your intent and see if it matched the course of nature
It could of been protecting you from danger
Instead of holding on to the rejection
You just need a small moment for reflection
Then you need to keep flowing
Keep going
One "no" is just a possible "yes" in the future
Don't just let one "no" stop you in your tracks
There is always opportunity hidden in the cracks
Don't let this consume you whole
Like a black hole
Instead reflect and radiate action
What is meant to be will in due time will always happen
Sometimes they say the ego wants things to happen quickly while the spirit knows what is meant will last an eternity

Don't give up because of one "no"
Rejection
Is just redirection
When reflection meets perfection
It was for your protection
So you could eventually reach the golden section
No ego just free flow
Mind, thoughts, and fearlessly let go
It just your navigational redirection
A new map to a greater destination

Courageous

Walking on the yellow brick road
Trying to find a way back home
Lost in the mix
Trying to heal all that needs to be fixed
Pain and struggles led to this place
Trapped and stuck in this crazy race
Surrounded by distractions
No additions just subtractions
Finally stirring up my chest of emotions
In a hypnotic trance I drank the wrong potion
Following everyone else off the path
Snapped out and realized I must finally give myself a chance
To stand
Stand for what I believe
Courage
Lioness
Sparkly shoes
Shimmering
Clinking together wishing I could get home
But, so far it felt
Nowhere to go
Home was always in my heart
Drawing me back
I had to keep going
Knowing

That there was a great chance
To make it back
It was all in how I chose to react
To stand
To be tall
To not let the opposition make me fall
For the courage had to build
To yield even when the power gave me chills
I had to face all my fears
Even when I was shedding tears
Not run away
Fight through every predator to not become prey
It was not a game to play
I was meant to get through it all to find my way
To fight
To be strong
Not mark defeat even when it felt all wrong
I had to maintain
Not go insane
Find a way to be courageous again
Continuous cycle
Fight for my beliefs
For I am the chief
I run this now
No lions, tigers, and bears just a queen with no more fears
There is a land I heard of home warm where the sky is always blue

No more clouds just happy faces euphoric places
Beyond the stars
Where all wounds and scars disappear
Over the rainbow you must go
To wash away your troubles and let them go
To hear the birds sing
Over and over the rainbow you must go
Courageously finding your way home

The moment we are timeless

That pure moment
Everything stops
Things are moving in slow motion
Time is suspended
Where legends are born
Because that suspension is timeless
Time which keeps ticking is no longer
It's frozen
Floating on clouds
Absence of sounds
Clarity creeps
Motivating greatness seeps
Whispering your next move
As instinct
Destined
No matter the direction
The outcome is always the same
So no need to rush for fame
That life is a game
For Ponds
Not Kings and Queens
The rush is not meant for preservation of humanity
Forgetting the blood we were all given
The options to choose us, we are all so human
Forgotten
By Greed

And ego
For that moment we are TIMELESS
Not centering our gravity around our universe to become
selfless
Defines hero's
A true human being

Hope

Holding on to something
It's hard to define it
Always there
Prescribed to all
HOPE
It is a feeling that beats in our soul
No matter the outcome there is always hope
Feeling lost, down, sad but hope is what transcends through all situations
Without any explanation
It just does
We make every move so complicated when we need to make it simple
It feels like a world of walking hurt people
That needs a large dose of hope
Through all hardships knowing it is around the corner helps us cope
For it gives us a glimpse of light and warmth we never imagined
Radiant feelings of satisfaction
For all is lost when there is no hope
We can see it in the glare of someone's eye as they lose it
But, it can be one event or moment to reignite and spark it
Hope is the desire for great impact and change for the positive
Releasing the negative

Letting it go
So hope can increase and grow
From seeds to acres of dreams
Always seek hope in everything
It exists
Don't give up on it
It's always there if you just find it
Smile
Keep your head high
Today is a new day to try
What is lost can be found
Hope is now

Dream Puff

A mini dream
Dream Puff
Lands slowly near your window
Time escapes
Doesn't matter
For that dream
Daydream is transcending through
Where all is possible
And can be true
It is determined by your belief
The desire to achieve
Something way stronger than the physical
Into another dimension of metaphysical
Pushed and pulled in directions never imagined
Imagination and creativity burst
Painting the dream you thought was impossible
Just that dream puff
It is possible
Keep dreaming and it will happen
Close your eyes and listen to your souls magic
It will happen in a puff and you won't be able to keep up
Keep your eyes open for the ride
Listen to the whispers and you will find
Your dream puff
It taste so good

Angel in the outfield

I feel you
Touching my heart
You are at a distance
So many can't hear or see you
But, I feel you
Are they blind to an angel's touch
Or was it designed that way
Helping so many as a guide
Designed to not be seen and just hide from the human eye
The touch ever so magical
Heavenly
Curing me
From all that's hurting
This dimension is for you to get your wings to heaven
To be a blessing
It's the last wish you have before you must go into the
next dimension
And on to your ascension
The gates await
Thankful for you watching and being my blessing
I remember that time you made my shirt get caught in the
door
To slow me down to the dangers
More Aware
You are here
All the magical things you have done are not forgotten

Mini blessings
Learning lessons
For you are my angel
In the outfield
Touching my heart
And those around me
I know how much you care
I wish you were physically here
Missing your presence in the flesh, but feeling your vibe everywhere
My angel in the outfield
Helping me plant seeds of greatness
You just never know what miracles can grow

Let me be your wings

Let me hold you up when your down
In the darkness of night
I will be that shooting star shining bright
Illuminating a path of hope
Assuring you to stay strong and cope
I am there for you
When you are falling back
My hands catch you
In a jam
My presence is here
Here I am
Being your wings
To help you fly
Kindness and love spreading you can't deny
For it is a smile that catches your eye
Spreading like wildfire
Your angelic light amplifier
For happiness is the key
Keeping your heartbeat
In motion
I'm here for you
A miracle being
Unexpectedly
Surprising you with great things
A gift
Helping you glide

Just a simple guide
Let me be your wings
So you can take that leap of faith and fly

Enthusiasm

Can't contain myself
Out of control crazy
Excitement
It's about to happen
Uncontrollable smiles
Frozen in time
Enthusiasm relentlessly cloaked
In Greek means "filled with God"
For enthusiasm fights to problem solve
To beat all odds
Turning fear
Into a new goddess of fierce
That lies within your chest
Pulling out your greatness and your best
It's in there
It's about to appear
If you just cut ties from the fear
And recognize your talents are right here
Embrace
Not chase
It's here to stay
Keep your enthusiasm and just play
Watch as the growth and fun turn you into a fearless renegade
Play
Pray

Slay
Enthusiastic vibes to serenade
Good vibes and times ready to invade
On that mind-shift upgrade

Manifesting

There is a saying it's all in your hands
Question is whether that is true
Forces are constantly pulling at you
Shifting your direction and attention
But, a true soul always knows their intentions
Leads to desires that are pure
Love, peace, and happiness is the cure
For what we believe we become
Our actions speak for all we have overcome
Our intent is our blessing
Our purpose is our torch
That lights up the sky
Like shooting stars in the night
Manifesting dreams to come true
It's all in what you say and what you do
Let your heart be your paintbrush
Keep painting with passion
For real truth organically rings
So do your thing
Manifesting

Lead with Love

Sometimes we lose our inner leader
We lost the light
We know it can shine bright
It gets lost in drama of mixed emotions
Toxic potions roaming in our minds
Telling us we are out of our minds
Truth is don't let someone roll up on your summer
Your summer is a perfect sunny day
You can't change anything when it rains
But, you can control the role it plays
On your heart and spirit
For all news has it's effects
Fake or not
We have the choice
To lead with fear or love
Two four letter words that can shift a paradigm and change the world
From your universe to universal
Dimension shifting
But, you make the choice in every word and action you speak upon
The drama that can't be undone
But, the start is now
Lead with love
There is simply no need for a how
It already is whispering to your heart

You already know how to start
Lead, lead, lead that love
Straight from the heart
A vessel of change
So many levels and stages
Seek kindness in every phase
For we all have some darkness and that one person to shine light can help
Be that flashlight for someone in need to see out of the dark
Leading with your love is the spark
Whispering moments woven from your truest of hearts
Never stop leading
This world is needing
Of your splash of love
Pulsing from your heart

New memories

It's easy to get caught up on what happened
The past is like chasing your tail
A circle trail
Never ending cycle
Let it all go
A new day
Is a fresh way
To clear time wasted away
Make room to play
A new chance for memories
The past which was once fun
Is now the shooting gun
Killing your current vibe and moment
For this instant
Is meant to be a clean slate to create
Not hold on or harbor
All that past
Shed it
Release it
For new is on its way
A horizon of great
You just have to make way
To create new memories

Time traveler

Time keeps ticking
Trying to blast to the future keeps itching
What if you could travel time
What would your past tell your present and could the future contact you
It exists time travel is true
For today your past is telling your present what happened to protect you in your future
So if we could write a note
This is no joke
What would we say
Would it be let loose more and play
Don't get held up in the past
Set yourself wild and free
Get that lotto ticket
Hug your family more
Tell your loved ones how much they mean to you
Invest in that stock that tripled
Buy real estate
Not hesitate
Fall in deep love
Be kind to everyone
What is stopping you
Your future is still being written by your past and present
So write this note now
And put it to action

For traveling time is happening
Happening right now at this very moment
Past telling your present
Be present
It's all in your energy and presence
Your future is up to what you write and what you tell yourself
You are a time traveler
Transcending time constantly
It's your vibration that shifts and changes
Your heart healing and bending through time
For time is continuous it's just dependent on how you want to live in that timeline
Past present future
Time is all in the beholder
Write your way through time
Creating your legacy in multiple dimensions is your paradigm
All possible in your Delorean of dreams
The future is a reflection in the light beams
The past can make it hard, but your choice to write a new lane taking you from rags to riches that will take you far
Beyond the stars
To another planet
As time is writing your habits
You must understand it
You are in control

Past present future
Woven together to make you whole
A whole new time traveler

Brave

Before in the past I looked at the mirror
I saw defeat
Scares, bruises, and wounds
Afraid for anyone to see
Someone frail
That always held on to the sadness in the fail
Grasping on like a life vest
Barely holding on to a lifeline
Walking and sulking in my sorrows
Feeling time was only borrowed and must be returned
It wasn't purchase
I was an imposter in my own body
Trying to be someone for everybody
Trapped in everyone else's thoughts
Not establishing my own
A reincarnation took form
As a butterfly came out of it's cocoon
All of a sudden purpose took over
Digging deep in one's heart
No better way then to restart
To build
Thought by thought
Brick by brick
Courage
Standing tall
Facing Fears

Being bold
Igniting visions
Creating dreams
Brave
Witnessing
Finally fighting for me
With every ounce in my body
Every thought radiating positivity
For this is a new day
To take the stage
And own it
Looking at flaws as blessings in disguise
Lessons and failures as guides
To be better than before
Push boundaries that can not be seen by the human eye
For you no longer are willing to hide that disguise
Shattering the past mirror reflection
Shedding that old skin
The reflection no longer subject to anyone else's thoughts
of you
All that matters is the fierce belief in you
To be brave in one's skin and take on the world
A truest form of a hero
Is the one who accepts themselves
And holds it in the fiercest way
Owns the praise
Because being brave

It's not easy
It's so scary
Fear always lurking to keep you stagnant
But, what is scarier is not living free
Held in everyone else subjectivity
Blurred lines of TMZ
And stories that aren't true
Media and perspectives will always make your face turn blue
If you believe them all just like fake news
You will be hostage to everyone else again
So why let the cycle begin
Ignore, block, and move on
Bravery for it takes shape to grows for someone to genuinely be themselves holds the realest truth
To set records like Babe Ruth
To inspire youth
It all takes a step out
To be bold
Not get stuck in everyone's mold
To challenge the status quo
Not keep up with the Jones or Kardashians
Who are they?
Snapchat and Instagram time suckers who hunt on the prey
Falling victim to its time waste
Be you
Keep creating your masterpieces

Make your own rules to break
Ignore the fake
Be your own icing on a cake
Keep shining
Inner motivation
No hesitation
Step out
Shout out
It is your time
Be brave

Soul digger

Down the rabbit hole you must go
To a place unknown
Where all the seeds and flowers take watering to grow
It's deep within
Where all your greatness can begin
It's takes time
Even when you want it so instant
It can happen in an instant
It just takes patience
As it is the several miracles that build to a big explosion
Of the unexpected
Dig deeper to your soul
You purpose never gets old
Ageless
Transcends time to get to your greatness
Keep moving
Into the movement
Keep doing
Creating
Dig deeper find your strength to push past the impossible
Showing dreams are possible
Put your words into action
Ignore the reactions
Because they are not on your level
Dead weights must Go
Fearless

Soulful
Magical
You
Soul digger

Glitter

It shines when the sun hits it
It even captures the dimmest of light
It always shimmers
It's your inner glitter
Let loose of the negative stop being bitter
Just shine be radiate glitter
It's not always easy
Nor breezy
But, the best way is to focus on what makes you smile and what makes you shine
For we all have a light so bright
It will always shine in the dimmest of night
Positive vibes and focus on how great you really are
You are a shining star
Let yourself glitter out
Show the world what you are about
It just may get everywhere

Be the best version of you

Searching deep into google
Self improvement
Self help
Self taught
Not bought
That best version
Lies within
You hold the pen
To write all your legacies
To search and find the best version of you
We are continually learning
Growing
Flourishing
Not knowing what great things are around the corner
But, what we can do is strive to find our best
To beat our best
The only competition that matters
Is being and beating your best yesterday
For everyday
Is a new day
A chance to laugh in the rain
Open one's once closed heart
Be open about our wounds and scars
To improve
Yesterday I messed up
But, today I learned from the past to be better

So life can get lighter not heavier
Releasing all these pressures
As magazines and posts don't define you
Let them inspire you
The real competition is standing in front of the mirror before you
To out beat yourself another day
To keep trying to be better in every way
There is time
You have the best version within you
To break the odds and do what lies true
It's all a part of a process
Life is cycles, from it's ups and downs
Smiles and frowns, the best yet to come
The journey is a long and winding road
But, truth be told
It's the little miracles and blessings along
That make you realize the improvement that can take place
And you had to experience everything you did
Even when it made you feel like you were in outer space
To make you the best version you could ever be
A game changer
About to rock and make history
It's time to take that torch and torque
Be best version you
In pursuit of life, love, happiness, and liberty

Find your slice of heaven

Imagine that piece of cake
Icing
Sweet thoughts and good feelings
It's just a matter of believing
That slice of heaven awaits
Ready to open it's pearly gates
For these goddess thoughts
Can't be bought
They are feelings
Cloaked in goodness
Smiles
Happiness
Turning your low into a major high
Euphoric feeling you can't deny
On that cake frosting and all
From the depths of hell
To the heavens
Your slice awaits
It had to happen that way
It was hard
Came out scarred and bruised
Healing had to occur
It's always a journey
Patience
Practice
Persistence

Facing fears and resistance
For that slice is going to be so good
It won't matter all the bad things that had to happen
For you stood through all tests
And now you will get your slice as you have proven to be at your best
Keep going and let your purpose come from your chest
Hearts speak and love can attest
Your slice of heaven is here
Remove your guilt or fear
As your vibe will elevate higher to see clear
You are meant to be just where you are, right here
So time to open your ears and hear
Heaven is near
That slice is on its way
So make way for all the blessings to open those gates
Opportunities and greatness awaits
Grab your fork and napkin
As all the magic is about to happen

About the poet

Lori Moilov is a poet and artist from Los Angeles, CA. She works on media content and production. She has worked for several networks and studios in entertainment; including BET, Robert Evans Company at Paramount, HBO, Lifetime, CBS, E!, G4, Showtime, Screen Gems, Sony, Disney, and many more.

Her passion is in the arts as a storyteller and supporting fellow artists in all mediums. She made the leap into producing making a short film "Power of Love." She continues to develop stories, poems, songwriting, and music records with a "PURPOSE."

She spends all her time being creative, writing, drone flying, photography, dancing, surfing, performing, and shooting cinematography.

When she is not being creative she loves being at the beach songwriting, surfing, skateboarding, and meditating to the waves. Her goal with all her creative endeavors is to be that glitter on a page, that initial spark that ignites creativity for others, while telling great inspiring stories that explore and evoke emotions.

Now it is your time to sparkle...

Believe in your inner glitter and shine, baby, shine!

www.ingramcontent.com/pod-product-compliance
Lightning Source LLC
Chambersburg PA
CBHW032116090426
42743CB00007B/376